Gangs
Deal with it
before wrong
seems right

Jabari Lindsay • Illustrated by Bjoern Arthurs

James Lorimer & Company Ltd., Publishers
Toronto

Gangs might be something you've only ever heard about . . .

Or maybe you know someone who is in a gang. Maybe there are gangs in your school or neighbourhood. You might even have personal experience with a gang. Either way, gangs are very real and can have a wide variety of definitions — and consequences.

Sometimes friends that hang out together a lot and who share the same interests and style of dress can seem as impenetrable as a gang when you are on the outside looking in. Being on the outside can make you think that anything would be better than being alone.

But think again.

If you're someone who doesn't have a lot of close friends or family, or if you feel like you don't really fit in, a gang can be a tempting way to make you feel better about yourself. Gangs seem to offer a sense of belonging and an instant group of friends who always have each other's back.

This is where things can change and become dangerous.

A gang is a group of people who are loyal to each other only on the surface. Gang members have to follow the same set of rules, no matter what. This leads to deep trouble when drugs, alcohol, or violence are used to maintain loyalty, keep members in line, or reach a perceived common goal.

Belonging to a group and belonging to a gang are two different things.

Gangs aren't just in big cities, nor are they what you see on TV or in movies. This book can help you understand the risks involved with gangs — so you can deal with them before wrong seems like the right thing to do.

Contents

What is a Gang?

Sometimes it can be hard to tell the difference between a gang and a group. At one time, the word "gang" simply meant a group of friends, or even a group of workers. But now there is a big difference between a **GANG** and a **GROUP**. Here are some of those differences.

GROUPS are made up of three or more people who:

- share the same race, ethnicity, religion, or neighbourhood, but could also be friends, work or go to school together, or enjoy the same hobbies
- might dress, act, or talk the same way to show they are part of the same group
- are like-minded, or have similar opinions
- abide by society's laws, rather than reject them
- respect each other's individuality
- do not define themselves by their enemies
- do not define themselves by illegal or criminal activities
- do not use bullying or intimidation tactics to keep members of the group in line
- are allowed to join or leave when they want, without fear of negative consequences or punishment

GANGS are a group of three or more people who:

- could have the same race, ethnicity, religion, or neighbourhood
- share a common goal or belief system that is their own
  - have their own rules and laws, which apply only to them
    - have a clearly defined leader and hierarchy
    - use people's weaknesses, such as poverty or loneliness, to entice them to join
- control what their members wear and who they hang out with
- have clearly defined enemies

Loyalty to a gang overrides the good of society and the good of its individual members. Loyalty to a group does not.

Gangs 101

People join gangs for . . .

MONEY

PROTECTION

FAMILY

FRIENDSHIP

QUIZ

At times we may question whether a group is really a gang, but by the time we learn the truth, we can be in too deep. Or we may think a group of friends is a gang, when really it isn't. Knowing the characteristics of groups and gangs can help us navigate situations better. You decide if each of the following is describing a GROUP or a GANG.

High Tops: GROUP or GANG?

1 All members of the High Tops listen to hip hop.

Group. Hip hop or rap music is a form of music often associated with gangs, but many gang members listen to a wide variety of music and many non-gang members like hip hop.

Raiders: GROUP or GANG?

2 All the members of the Raiders wear black.

Group. Many sports teams use all black to intimidate their opponents. Although in many towns, team colours can be the same as a gang's colours. If you're not allowed to wear anything else for fear of violence, then it's a gang. Anything else is a group.

Flaming Js: GROUP or GANG?

3 Johnny and Jimmy call themselves the Flaming Js. They sell drugs and rob people.

Group. Even though they do gang-related activities, they are too small to be a gang. They need more people. They may try to target you, showing you all the fun they are having to try and recruit you, but with only two people, they are still a group.

Outlaws: GROUP or GANG?

4 All the members of the Outlaws trade illegal weapons.

Gang. There is no question here. The key is that they are trading illegal weapons. Most gang members carry weapons because they see themselves as being at war.

Snakes: GROUP or GANG?

5 All the members of the Snakes are the same race.

Group. Many cultural groups come together to celebrate their race. When these groups spend time in parks or in their neighbourhood, people may not like it and through fear start calling them a gang, but they are a group.

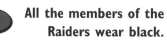

Clobbers: GROUP or GANG?

 All the members of the Clobbers have a secret handshake that only they know how to do.

Group. Any group of people can have a handshake that they all do. This doesn't make them a gang.

Hawks: GROUP or GANG?

 All the members of the Hawks believe in money over other people.

Gang. Most gang members are highly motivated to get money by any means necessary.

Pan Crew: GROUP or GANG?

 All the members of the Pan Crew have a tattoo depicting their group's logo.

Gang. Any group that asks you to get a tattoo that depicts the group is usually a gang. Many friends or people from the same culture can get tattoos that are similar, but no one should force you to into getting a tattoo of any sort.

Royales: GROUP or GANG?

 All the members of the Royales choose loyalty to each other over obeying the rules.

Gang. Loyalty is the most important thing in a gang. You may even have to choose your gang over your family.

Flores: GROUP or GANG?

 All the members of the Flores penalize members who leave their group.

Gang. Gang members who decide to leave the gang may face severe consequences that could end up hurting them or their families. Or both.

**What's your crew?
GROUP or GANG?**

Dear Gang Counsellor

Q: It seems to me that most gang members are happy and rich, so why wouldn't I want to be part of a gang too?

— *Wannabe*

A: Record companies and the media have been glorifying the image of gang members turned into rich, successful hip hop artists for a long time. In reality, most gang members come from difficult and stressful conditions and would have chosen another way of life if they'd felt there were other options available to them. If you are not happy, there are many choices and options that can lead you down a path of success without having to join a gang. Talk to an adult you trust who is happy and successful and ask how he or she got to where they are — I bet it wasn't through a gang.

Q: I'm in Boy Scouts and play on a hockey team, and my sister is part of the glee club. I don't get what the big difference is between our groups and street gangs. I mean, they're all groups of people who have certain things in common, right?

— *In Denial*

A: It's true that people who join groups like sports teams or special-interest clubs seem to do so for similar reasons that a person would join a street gang. The difference is that people who join Boy Scouts, hockey teams, or glee clubs do it for enjoyment and to try to be a positive member of their community. People who join street gangs are only concerned with the good of their gang — often at the expense of their community.

Q: I have a friend at school who I just found out is part of a gang. I'm not sure how to treat him now. Are gang members really bad people?

— *Conflicted*

A: Gang members are people like you and me. Unfortunately, they have decided or been forced to make bad choices. They feel like they have no other options and are driven by things like money and power. I'm happy you asked this question because it tells me you are looking for the good in people. Keep making good choices, and if you know someone who is in a gang, help him or her to make good personal choices too.

Q: It seems that every time I see a gang member on TV or in the news he's black. Are all gang members black?

— *Colour Blind*

A: There are some gangs that were first formed based on race or ethnicity. In fact, many of these particular gangs were started to help people from that race get ahead in life. Sometimes people of a certain race or background are treated unfairly in society and live in poverty or in other difficult situations. This is wrong, but starting a street gang isn't the solution. At their core, gangs don't really care about someone's ethnicity as much as their availability and willingness to do things that will benefit the gang.

Myths

Gang members have each others' backs — always!

While some people believe that joining a gang will protect them from bullies or other gang members, being in a gang greatly increases the chances of being a target for rival gangs.

A gang is just like a family.

Real families accept and love one another for who they are. If someone is having problems in his or her family, joining a gang will not help — it will only make things worse. Don't be fooled: even if members of your biological family are gang members, joining the gang does not create an extended family for you.

Joining a gang means having lots of friends.

A gang may not approve of friends or dating outside the gang. They may question and test loyalty by insisting that members hang out only with each other.

Gang members get a lot of respect.

Respect in gang culture goes away the first time a member fails to do what the gang has told them to do. Gang respect isn't real, and it doesn't last.

DID YOU KNOW?

- The Prairie region of Canada has 108 different gangs.
- The Greater Toronto Area has 137 different gangs.

DEAR DR. SHRINK-WRAPPED...

Q: I was walking home when a group of kids from my school asked me to draw a symbol on the side of my school. They showed me what it looks like and the symbol doesn't look bad; it actually kind of represents my history and culture. Should I just do it?

— *Can in Hand*

A: Some gangs will get you to do something that seems like it's no big deal as part of an early initiation. But once you take the first step, they will try and get you to do more dangerous things and will threaten to tell on you if you don't do what they say. Take Dr. Shrink-Wrapped's advice: Tell them that the symbol looks awesome but that you're not into drawing on buildings. Walk away.

Q: There is no food in the fridge, I wear the same clothes every day, and most of the people in my community are in a similar situation. One group of kids has decided to start robbing people to make money. My friends and I are being offered "positions" as lookouts. They say we are smart and want us to help. What should I do?

— *Sick and Tired of Being Sick and Tired*

A: To even ask this question you are quite brave. But one thing Dr. Shrink-Wrapped knows is this: If you decide to join your friends in this life of crime, it can only end badly. Victims of these robberies may become your enemies afterwards, and they may use violence to try to take back their belongings. The older kids are trying not to get caught, so they are asking you to get in trouble for them by becoming lookouts. A criminal record is no joke. It can ruin your life when you get older. I can see why it is difficult to make a positive choice in this situation, but you don't have to make it alone. Find an adult in your life who might be able to give you options that do not involve taking things from other people.

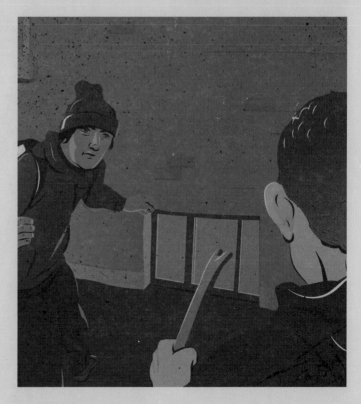

QUIZ

What's it gonna be?

Maybe you already know what your attitude is towards gangs. Are you DOWN with the idea? Or maybe you're GONE as soon as a gang situation arises. Perhaps you DON'T KNOW for sure where you're at. Better take this next quiz to find out . . .

I'm Down

I'm Gone

Who Knows?

1

The newest multiplayer game is out and you're tired of hearing about how intense last night's battles were. All you need is $60 to join in the fun. Some guys you know can show you how to make that much money in a day.

What's it gonna be?

I'm Down   I'm Gone   Who Knows?

2

You're upset. This is the fourth year in a row that your dad has forgotten to call you on your birthday. Your friends say smoking weed is a good way to forget your troubles.

What's it gonna be?

I'm Down   I'm Gone   Who Knows?

3

Your older brothers were always your protectors growing up. Now they're both in a gang and they need you to do them a favour in return.

What's it gonna be?

I'm Down   I'm Gone   Who Knows?

4

You get good grades, go to school every day, and stay out of trouble. Now you're tempted to join a gang, since it won't matter if you get into trouble because you've had a clean record up until now.

What's it gonna be?

I'm Down   I'm Gone   Who Knows?

5

Your family doesn't have much money and you feel like you should help bring money into your household. Getting fast, illegal money is an option.

What's it gonna be?

I'm Down   I'm Gone   Who Knows?

6

Usually you go home after school to watch your favourite TV show and relax, then maybe do some homework. Today your friends are asking you to stay late and help them in a fight.

What's it gonna be?

I'm Down   I'm Gone   Who Knows?

7

You've always dreamed of becoming a teacher. One of your friends tells you to forget about it and focus on how to get in with her older brother and his gang. That's where the money is, she says.

What's it gonna be?

I'm Down   I'm Gone   Who Knows?

8

You don't feel like your school or community accepts people of your race. A person tells you that if you join them, you will get the respect you deserve.

What's it gonna be?

I'm Down   I'm Gone   Who Knows?

9

It's your first day at a new school and you're wearing the t-shirt your aunt got you. It's your favourite colour. A kid approaches and tells you to take off the shirt because that colour isn't allowed on your school's turf.

What's it gonna be?

I'm Down   I'm Gone   Who Knows?

10

A friend of yours is in a gang and gets shot. You're told by some of his "new friends" that if you were a real friend, you would join them to help get even.

What's it gonna be?

I'm Down   I'm Gone   Who Knows?

So you're **thinking** of **joining** the **gang?**

Ok, maybe not joining, but maybe just spending time with them. After all, you've known some of these kids since your playground days. But before you go, think about this . . .

Realize that the consequences for gang members can affect those closest to them. Just because you're not a member doesn't mean that the police won't arrest you or that the gang's enemies won't try and shoot you too. To stay safe, the only option is to stay away.

There are plenty of positive activities you could be doing! Try them all before you try the gang life. Try out for all the sports teams your school has to offer, get straight As for a full year, or maybe volunteer for a summer. Once you begin to do these things you will be too busy to hang out with gangs.

Go back and look at the myths on pages 12 and 13. Are you getting caught up in these dreams?

DID YOU KNOW?

• Hundreds of kids choose to join gangs every year, and hundreds of kids get hurt or die from gang violence every year.

dos and don'ts

✓ Do look for other things to do.

✓ Do chase your dreams.

✓ Do your own thing.

✓ Do physical activity; it will make you feel good.

✓ Do resist all temptations to join a gang, even if it seems to be a good thing.

Not being part of a gang doesn't mean you have to be a loner. Spend time with whomever you want but always remember you have the choice to walk away. If you feel like that choice is gone, you shouldn't be with those people.

✗ Don't believe in any of the benefits of gangs.

✗ Don't spend time with gang members.

✗ Don't hang out doing nothing all day, every day.

✗ Don't neglect your school work — education is key.

✗ Don't get into the lifestyle of a gang member — it's really hard to get out of.

- Jail is a common destination for gang members.
- Girls who become gang members have the same risks as guys.

- Youth as young as 8 years old are recruited into gangs.
- Graffiti can be gang related but not all graffiti is done by gangs.

You're **living** the life you **always wanted**, on your way to being part of the **biggest crew** in town.

It doesn't matter how you got there. Maybe a few people hate you now, but that's cool; they're not worth your time anymore.

Yet... it still **doesn't feel right.**

Your reasons for joining don't seem important anymore and leaving is no longer an option. Or is it? **As an Insider there are ways to get out.**

dos and don'ts

✓ Do stay in school; it's the only real way to make it.

✓ Do understand that being in a gang is dangerous and stressful.

✓ Do tell an adult what you're going through.

✓ Do realize there are positive groups in your neighbourhood to join.

✗ Don't be bullied; stand up for yourself.

✗ Don't pressure others to join.

✗ Don't believe that crime is a good way to live.

✗ Don't stop believing in a positive future.

✗ Don't be afraid to ask for advice.

✗ Don't follow bad friends; they won't be there when you really need them.

✓ Do research on what your gang stands for — you may not agree with it.

✓ Do create a dream for yourself and follow it.

QUIZ

Is it time for me to leave my gang?

The world isn't easy to figure out, but when all the answers to your questions suggest you're in a bad place, you usually are. You may not think your gang is bad, but if you answer YES to more than 10 of the following statements, then you need to think again and start thinking about your gang exit strategy right now!

1. Whenever we are together we tend to get in trouble.

2. I do bad things when I'm with my friends.

3. I get sent home from school a lot.

4. The "good" kids are afraid of me.

5. My parents say they are worried about me.

6. My parents say they have no clue what I'm up to.

7. I get into fights because of my friends.

8. My friends get me to sell drugs or keep their weapons in a safe place for them.

9. My friends make me watch out for police while they do things.

10. I don't like feeling alone so I hang out with my friends.

11. I don't like being picked on so I hang out with my friends.

12. I never have enough money or food so I try and get it with my friends.

13. All of my role models are gang members.

14. The music I listen to says it's cool to be in a gang.

15. I draw symbols that represent my group on everything.

16 I wear the same colours all the time.

17 If I saw one of the members of my group do something bad, I would never tell on them.

18 I don't snitch.

19 I like treating people badly.

20 I enjoy making money.

21 I enjoy smoking or drinking.

22 People who are not part of my group are losers.

 23 Jail seems like a cool place, and I wouldn't mind going.

 24 The only way to make it in my community is to join a gang.

 25 One day my group will let me hold a gun just like they do on TV.

 26 People say I look like a gang member.

27 I bully people who are not part of my gang.

28 I want to get rich or die trying.

Your pot is boiling over!

You've been in one too many **fights** and you've seen **really bad things** happen to people. You **want to leave** this gang, but you're not sure how to do it. **DON'T WAIT!** The time to **leave** the gang is **now**. Here are some tips to begin planning your way out:

Don't tell any of your gang brothers and sisters of your decision. They may think you are deciding to turn on them and do you harm. Instead, work on becoming comfortable with the decision yourself, and create your own process.

Stop doing gang-related activity as soon as possible. You may still see your homies around but not engaging in gang-related activities will keep you safe as you build your new life.

Start spending time doing positive social activities: sports, clubs, and other after-school activities. These will keep you busy and give you an excuse to say no when your homies ask you to do things with them.

Create a list of excuses to use if your homies call or catch you on the street. Practice them to make sure they are believable.

DID YOU KNOW?

Male Gang Facts

• 90% are arrested by age 18.
• 75% are arrested twice by age

Girls and Gangs

Many people believe that gangs only have guys in them. Wrong! Girls can join gangs too. They offer the same benefits for males who join gangs, like excitement, meeting new people, making money, and providing a sense of safety. Girls may also join a gang to find a new family if their home is full of sadness. Once a girl joins a gang she may be used as the mother figure or as a slave to the men. She no longer has a voice and can be used until the guys don't want her anymore. To solve this issue, some girls create their own gangs. But this isn't the best answer because it can pose other risks, such as jail and violence.

The most common victims of gang violence are the girlfriends of gang members. The gang members are most often the target of a shooting, but it's the girlfriends who can be shot instead.

Everything you have learned in this book applies to girls and gangs as well as to boys.

Stand up for yourself.
Making this choice will be a hard one. It will be the hardest choice you will ever have to make. Your friends will try to make fun of you and may even threaten you, but remember, your REAL friends would never make you do something you didn't want to do.

- 95% do not finish high school.
- 60% are dead or in prison by age 20.

- The average life expectancy of an active gang member is 20 years, five months.

The **Witness**

You may have noticed that the kids in your school or neighbourhood have begun to choose sides.

They are choosing groups who have names like "Bloods" or "Crips." You see your close friends choosing and people are beginning to ask you,

"What side are you on?"

It's okay to not pick a side when it comes to choosing between gangs.

It may feel like you're alone at first, but it won't last long. Before you know it, people may choose to hang with you because all that gang stuff is so stressful.

dos and don'ts

✓ Do realize that you're in a better position to help someone by staying outside of a gang, rather than by being in one.

✓ Do speak up if you feel it's safe to do so.

✓ Do ask an adult for help if you know someone is in trouble or being pressured to join a gang.

✓ Do take positive action in your community to stop gang violence.

✓ Do walk away from negative situations rather than start a confrontation.

✓ Do take a stand and tell people you are on your own side and search for others who are interested in doing the same thing, even if it is a small group of people.

✓ Do stay positive and continue to make positive choices.

✗ Don't choose a gang; that way you can keep your real choices open for your future.

✗ Don't do anything to challenge gang members directly.

✗ Don't wear gang colours or use gang symbols.

✗ Don't get involved in gang problems or warfare.

✗ Don't side with a gang out of loneliness.

QUIZ

Do you really get it?

Gangs can seem like the only way out for someone who feels he or she has no other options. But knowing that there are other choices can help someone in this position realize that there are better solutions than participating in a gang lifestyle. When it comes to gangs — whether it's something you've heard about, seen in your school or neighbourhood, or had direct experience with — understanding both sides of the situation will ensure that you can help make the best choices for your friends, family, or even yourself. So let's see if you really get it.

2 CASH GRAB

You know of a group of kids who rob other kids after school and they keep bugging you to do it with them. How will you respond?

- You know that people rob other people when they feel helpless to get it themselves, but you also know there are always better ways.
- They may be doing it to punish the victim, something that didn't involve you in the first place. Better to stay out of it.
- By keeping busy with other things, like Scouts, karate club, or the swim team, you won't be around for them to bug you.

1 POPULARITY CONTEST

It seems like all the cool kids in your school use drugs. You and your best friend have never done drugs, but your friend wants to be more popular and has been hanging out with them after school. How can you change her mind?

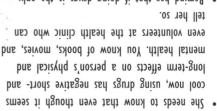

- She needs to know that even though it seems cool now, using drugs has negative short- and long-term effects on a person's physical and mental health. You know of books, movies, and even volunteers at the health clinic who can tell her so.
- Remind her that if doing drugs is the only thing she and her new friends do together, then it's not really a friendship.
- Tell her that since she's been doing drugs she hasn't seen as much of her family or her other friends and that you miss her.

③ FEAR FACTOR

Your cousin lives in a rough part of town. He tells you that there are two gangs at his school and the situation is getting scary. He wants to do something about it, but doesn't know what. What advice can you offer him?

- Your cousin can talk to his teacher about running an anti-gang campaign. Even signs and conversations can help people change their minds about being in a gang.
- Your cousin can ask his school if they can start a safe group for kids who don't want to be around when bad things happen. This will give them a place to go and people to turn to.
- Ask your cousin to do some research into having a guest speaker at your school. Lots of famous people had to make the tough choice about joining a gang. They may have some helpful advice.

④ Pay the Bills

Money is tight at home. Your brother told you that if he joined the gang in your neighbourhood they would help him get extra money. What do you do?

- Before you or your brother take that chance, try looking for a part-time job.
- Talk to your mom or dad about what you can do to help out around the house. It could be as simple as cutting back on unnecessary expenses, like giving up extra cable channels, to help the family out.
- Don't assume that getting money for the family is your responsibility. Doing well in school may be what is needed from you.

⑤ THE WAY OUT

You and Damion grew up together, but once he joined a gang, the two of you stopped talking. Now he's told you he is tired of being a gang member and wants out. He believes there's no hope! What can you do?

- It's difficult, but not impossible for Damion to get out. Be supportive and tell him that he can get help.
- Approaching a teacher or parent might be difficult for Damion. This is where you can take action.
- Don't tell any of the other kids about Damion's choice. He may not be ready for everybody to know and it could put him in danger.

Continues . . .

6 Payback

The kid who lives down the hall from you is always getting bullied. One day you see him getting an offer to help settle the score from the older guys at school, who you've seen hanging out with a street gang. Walking home together after school, you think of what you should tell your neighbour . . .

- You tell him he needs to remember that every time those bigger kids help him, he might then owe them something.
- You remind him that there may come a time when the bigger kids won't be there for him. What then?
- You tell him that talking to an adult he trusts at school or at home to deal with the bullying directly avoids having to go through a gang.

7 LOOKS GOOD TO ME ...

Your younger sister sees all the gangsters on TV. She can't see what's so bad about that lifestyle and argues that they seem to be happy and successful. What do you say to her?

- Gang clothing and gangster music is owned and controlled by music companies who are not gang members. They are selling an image, not reality.
- Listening to the music doesn't make you a gang member, but supporting gangs in any way does more harm than good.
- If you listen to positive music and watch positive shows you will have an easier time being happy and successful too!

8 Fly the Colours

Kids at your school are beginning to wear the colours of a gang that runs in your neighbourhood. None of them are really in the gang, but they wear it to make themselves feel safe and to seem cool. What should you do?

- Keep strong and wear what you want. Maybe planning a different route from school or staying with other kids is an option.
- The enemies of that gang won't know whether those kids are in the gang or not. If you dress like them, you may get the same treatment as them. It's not worth it.
- Being your own person is much cooler than copying other people.

⑩ TAKE CONTROL

Your friend is always fighting with her parents. She tells you she's thinking of joining the gang at your school so that her parents can't boss her around anymore. What do you say?

- Tell her that her parents want what's best for her. It may not seem that way sometimes, but she should try and talk with them to sort things out.
- Tell your friend to speak with a trusted adult outside of her family who can help her get through to her parents.
- Talk to your own parents and get advice from them. You never know — they may have been in a similar situation when they were your age. They might even be willing to help your friend out.

⑨ THE THING TO DO

Jessi has decided she wants no part of gang life. But she knows that in her neighbourhood things are always changing, and she knows that as she gets older things might change. What should she do to keep her promise to herself to stay free of gangs?

- Jessi's decision is great and she should tell the positive people in her life who will help her keep that promise to herself as she gets older.
- Right away Jessi should start deciding what she will do instead, like what sports she might play or working toward a career goal.
- Jessi is going to have to start making choices that will keep her safe, such as going home early or choosing another route home from school.

More Help

Steering clear of gangs can be a challenge. But there are lots of resources available to help you deal with gangs in your neighbourhood, school, or home, and for people who want to learn more about the realities of gang life. Here is a list of some of those resources.

Helplines
Kids Help Phone 1-800-668-6868
311 (non-emergency services)

Websites
Kids Help Phone: www.kidshelpphone.ca
Teen Central: www.teencentral.net
Youth Worker Training Initiative: http://ywti.org/
Bereaved Families of Toronto: www.bfotoronto.ca/programs/distress_numbers.asp
Befrienders Worldwide: www.befrienders.org/helplines/helplines.asp?c2=Canada

Books
The Price of Loyalty by Mike Castan. Holiday House, 2011.
Dirt Road Home by Watt Key. Farrar Straus Giroux, 2010.
Yummy by G. Neri and Randi DuBurke. Lee and Low Books, 2010.
See No Evil (Orca Currents) by Diane Young. Orca Book Publishers. 2006.
Monster by Walter Dean Myers. HarperCollins Publishers, 1999.
Drive-By by Lynne Ewing. HarperCollins Publishers, 1996.
Scorpions by Walter Dean Myers. HarperCollins Publishers, 1988.

Movies
Mouse, 2008 (www.mousethemovie.com).
Down for Life, 2009 (R).
Redemption: The Stan Tookie Williams Story, 2004 (TV).
Stryker, 2006.

Other Titles in the Deal With It series
Cliques: Deal with it using what you have inside by Kat Mototsune, illustrated by Ben Shannon
Image: Deal with it from the inside out by Kat Mototsune, illustrated by Ben Shannon
Peer Pressure: Deal with it without losing your cool by Elaine Slavens, illustrated by Ben Shannon
Bullying: Deal with it before push comes to shove by Elaine Slavens, illustrated by Brooke Kerrigan
Misconduct: Deal with it without bending the rules by Anne Marie Aikins, illustrated by Steven Murray

Text copyright © 2012 by Jabari Lindsay
Illustrations copyright © James Lorimer & Company Ltd., Publishers

James Lorimer & Company Ltd., Publishers, acknowledges the support of the Ontario Arts Council. We acknowledge the financial support of the Government of Canada through the Canada Book Fund for our publishing activities. We acknowledge the support of the Canada Council for the Arts which last year invested $24.3 million in writing and publishing throughout Canada. We acknowledge the Government of Ontario through the Ontario Media Development Corporation's Ontario Book Initiative.

Canada Council for the Arts   Conseil des Arts du Canada

ONTARIO ARTS COUNCIL
CONSEIL DES ARTS DE L'ONTARIO

Series design: Blair Kerrigan/Glyphics

Library and Archives Canada Cataloguing in Publication

Lindsay, Jabari
    Gangs : deal with it before wrong seems right / Jabari Lindsay ; illustrated by Bjoern Arthurs.

(Deal with it)
Issued also in an electronic format.
ISBN 978-1-55277-920-0 (bound).--ISBN 978-1-55277-917-0 (pbk.)

    1. Gangs--Juvenile literature. I. Arthurs, Bjoern II. Title. III. Series: Deal with it (Toronto, Ont.)

HV6437.L55 2012   j364.106'6   C2011-907307-?

James Lorimer & Company Ltd., Publishers
317 Adelaide Street West, Suite 1002
Toronto, ON, Canada
M5V 1P9
www.lorimer.ca

Distributed in the United States by:
Orca Book Publishers
P.O. Box 468, Custer, WA
USA 98240-0468

Printed and bound in China.

Manufactured by Everbest Printing Company Ltd. in Guangzhou, China in January 2012.
Job number: 105864